John's Jesus

The Message and Meaning of John's Gospel

John Proctor

Director of New Testament Studies,
Westminster College, Cambridge

GROVE BOOKS LIMITED

RIDLEY HALL RD CAMBRIDGE CB3 9HU

Contents

Preface

John writes both simply and deeply about Jesus, and his gospel has been a source of insight and delight to many. But most of these readers will never have time to be specialists. This booklet is for them. It aims to open up the gospel, to set out its main themes, and to show how it still speaks today.

I have learned from many a hefty tome on John, and acknowledge some of these debts in chapter 7. If this little book whets your appetite, you may want to look up some of these others.

A number of colleagues, including members of the Grove Biblical Group, have offered gracious and helpful comment as this work was being prepared.

The Cover Illustration is by Peter Ashton

First Impression June 2007
ISSN 1365-490X
ISBN 978 1 85174 657 6

Introduction

All four gospels are absorbing to read and study, and rich in the insight they give into God and his love.

But for many Christians John stands out. Its language seems simple and straightforward, yet the text is heavy with layers of meaning, allusion and echo. This gospel invests ordinary things of life with great symbolic significance, but without robbing them of their ordinariness. As John leads us through his story, we are filled with a profound sense of glory and grace. He tells us of the life of Jesus, in which we ourselves have a share.

John is certainly the most distinctive of the gospels. It roots the Jesus story in the very beginning of time (1.1–3). It portrays his ministry around a series of seven signs — miracles with meaning, selected to promote faith (20.30f). From early on there is action in Jerusalem and Judea (eg 2.13–3.21; 3.22–4.3), as well as in Galilee (2.1–12; 4.43–54). We meet long passages of conversation and debate (6.25–59; 8.12–59), and at times Jesus makes strong and direct claims about himself (6.35; 10.30; 14.6). Many an important incident from other gospels is missing (as Mark 14.22–25, Jesus' eucharistic words at the Last Supper), yet there is sometimes a resonance in an unexpected corner of John (6.51–59). Conversely some of John's best-known episodes appear in this gospel alone (2.1–11; 4.5–42).

John's gospel addresses the reader with striking clarity. Its repeated 'whoever' beckons you and me to trust Jesus too (3.16; 5.24; 7.37f; 11.25f). This gospel has intent and purpose. John wants to help people believe (20.31).

If we dissect John, it splits into two. The first half — the 'Book of Signs' — is a varied and busy account of miracles and teaching, of interest and controversy. Then at the start of John 13 the writing changes pace, and the second half is very focused. The cross has come clearly into view, and now it acts as a magnet for the story. This is the 'Book of the Passion' or 'Book of Glory.'[1] But this is not a complete and sudden switch of direction. There has been a steady movement towards the cross from the start of the gospel. Jesus' 'hour,' of which we heard long before, has now arrived (2.4; 7.30; 8.20; 12.23, 27; 13.1; 17.1).

On the edges of these two main sections, the first and last chapters serve as introduction and epilogue. John 1 places Jesus on the stage of Israel's history, and John 21 sets the disciples as Jesus' people in the world. In the pages ahead we explore these sections in closer detail.

2 The Overture to the Gospel

John 1: The Presence of the Scripture

John's gospel starts with a prologue—the first eighteen verses. After this comes an obvious change of tone. But the whole of the first chapter continues what the prologue has begun. It echoes Scripture, sets Jesus in context and helps us to understand him, before we see him at work. A number of Old Testament themes appear, to show the significance of the man whose career we are about to follow. He comes into Israel. He fulfils ideals and aspirations from her scripture. He gives new life to her heritage and hopes.

Jesus and Genesis

John opens his gospel by echoing the account of creation, from the start of Genesis. 'In the beginning,' says John, 'was the word' (1.1). Through the word all things came into being, and light shone in a dark world (1.3–5). This word of which John writes is God's powerful creative goodness, which once breathed across the earth, to form life out of formless void (Gen 1.1–5).

Thus far the prologue seems almost detached from time. Yet the lines about John the Baptist (1.6–8, 15) anchor these verses to a particular point in time and space. So when we eventually hear the name Jesus (1.17), we realize that the whole prologue is about him. He is the word, the light, the life-giver, the stranger. He is the Father's only Son, full of glory, grace and truth.[2]

For this gospel is not just re-telling the story of the world's ancient birth. Rather John thinks of a new kind of life, a fresh creative goodness brought by Jesus, to breathe light into the world's darkness and stir humanity to new birth. Creation is being remade from within.

The link to Genesis runs on. 'The next day' says John's text, 'that day, the third day' (1.29, 35, 39, 43; 2.1), as if imitating the seven days of creation (Gen 1.1–2.3).[3] The week ends at the Cana wedding, where man and woman are brought together with the wine of the gospel, in a foretaste of earth's final sabbath rest.

There may be a further biblical connection. The figure of wisdom is described in Proverbs as the one born first in creation, God's companion when the earth was made (Pr 3.19; 8.22–31). Like a child at the father's side (John 1.18), wisdom lived close to God (8.30). As hostess at a feast, she shares her wine with seeking souls (9.1–6).[4] In Jesus too, God's wise and loving purpose comes to feed and to teach us; the art and grace that shaped creation offers us life and peace (Pr 3.17f).

Jesus and the World

There is a painful paradox in John's prologue, which shapes much of the gospel ahead. 'Though the world owed its life to him, the world knew him not' (1.10). The earth the word had made made him a stranger. God will not cease loving the world (3.16); but it is a hostile place too, stubbornly unreceptive to the life and promise brought by Jesus (16.33). Heaven's love and earth's anger will not be easy neighbours; ultimately their tension will lead to the cross.

Indeed the life of Israel works out, on a narrower stage, the great drama of God and the world. The word's coming to 'his own' shrinks the focus. Israel too does not know him (1.11). Her people are drawn, with the rest of us, into an ambiguity of resistance and grace. What Jesus brings is rooted in their common life (4.22), but it may not find a ready welcome in their minds (3.10). The nexus of genes and custom that is Israel cannot easily contain the life of the word.

Israel cannot easily contain the life of the word

For Jesus gives life to those 'who believe in his name' (1.12). New birth does not depend on the regular chain of ancestry and procreation (1.13). It is a different process, transcending the usual links and limits of human community (3.5–8). Yet John is no narrowly spiritual gospel, detached from this physical world. The word has genuinely shared our being. God has taken mortal flesh, and we saw his glory (1.14)—in our history and our humanity.

Jesus and Moses

Amid the links to Genesis, comes an echo of the Exodus, as John's prologue recalls Moses' encounter with the Lord on Mount Sinai. 'Glory' is a common thread in both passages (John 1.14; Exodus 33.18, 22), as is the giving of the law (Jn 1.17; Ex 34.1–4). Jesus was 'full of grace and truth' (Jn 1.14, 17), just as God is 'rich in steadfast love and faithfulness' (Ex 34.6). A clear sight of God, never quite granted to Moses, has now been given the world in Jesus (Jn 1.18; Ex 33.20–23).

Certainly the two eras contrast. Moses carried God's word, and Jesus incarnated it (Jn 1.17). Yet this is not the contrast of light and shadow, still less of light and darkness; rather it is 'grace upon grace' (Jn 1.16). John's gospel handles the Old Testament positively, as a period hallowed by God, as a time of preparation, witness and hope.

Jesus and Passover

To introduce Moses is to approach the Passover, Israel's pilgrim festival of sacrifice and freedom, commemorating their release from Egypt. In contrast to the synoptic gospels, John mentions three Passovers. At the first we see Jesus as the Temple of God's presence (2.13ff). The second brings hints of the church's eucharist (6.4ff). And the third leads on to the cross (11.55ff), where Jesus, the Lamb of God, gathers the whole gospel story into the great Passover of his dying.

In John, as in other gospels, the prospect of Jesus' cross appears early in the story. 'Lamb of God' (1.29, 36) is a Passover image, of sacrifice and death. But the title also recalls Isaiah's words, where one is 'brought as a lamb to slaughter' for 'the iniquity of us all' (53.6f). As this servant would be 'lifted up and glorified' (Isaiah 52.13), John too uses these words, to speak of Jesus' crucifixion (3.14; 8.28; 12.32; and 12.23; 13.31). Indeed the figures of Passover lamb and suffering servant seem to coalesce at the cross.

Jesus and David
John uses the term 'kingdom of God' less than the synoptics do (only in John 3.3, 5). But there is a royal aura around Jesus. When John the Baptist speaks of the Spirit 'descending and resting' on Jesus (1.32f), we may think of the Spirit coming to the young king David (1 Sam 16.13), and of Isaiah's hope for a 'branch' from David's line on whom the Spirit of the Lord will 'rest' (Isaiah 11.1–2).

When Nathanael hears of Jesus (1.46), he is sceptical. Nazareth was an obscure place. But Hebrew is a consonantal language: nezer ('branch') and Nazareth had similar sounds. When Nathanael goes on to speak of kingship (1.49), is John hinting that Jesus of Nazareth is the 'branch' of Isaiah 11? He is on a royal mission, bringing God's rule to Israel in the Spirit's power.

Jesus and Jacob
Jacob, also named Israel, was the father of the twelve tribes. But he had been a trickster too. So when Jesus calls Nathanael 'an Israelite without guile' (1.47), this seems ironic. Perhaps Jacob is again on stage, but in new guise and with a new nature. Then the ladder appears (1.51; cf Gen 28.12), casting Jesus as the new Jacob—the contact point between heaven and earth, and Israel's source of new life.

The Presence of the Scripture
So John portrays Jesus against a rich biblical tapestry. He shows, from early in the gospel, that the word written and the word incarnate illuminate one another. He intends us, as we read on, to look for meaning in the things Jesus does, and to interpret these too in the light of Israel's ancient story. We shall meet again these OT connections we have traced.

The Jesus of Mission

3

John 2–4: The Honeymoon of the Ministry

Jesus' first two signs take place at Cana, not far from Nazareth (2.1–11; 4.46–54). In between come plenty of travel, and a series of incidents and conversations. This period of the gospel carries a sense of freshness and discovery. The discussions are probing, even challenging, but they fall short of the outright hostility we meet from John 5. And even at this early stage, the layers of meaning tumble over one another, to claim our attention.

Seeing with New Glasses (2.1–11)
The 'signs' in John are good in themselves, but they also point to deeper meaning. Always there is another level, behind or beneath the event itself. It may be significant that the first sign comes at a wedding feast, and the last follows a funeral (11.1–44). Jesus enters into a full spectrum of human experience, emotion and relationship. He rejoices and he weeps, with others (*cf* Rom 12.15). But why turn water into wine? One answer comes at 2.11: this is a glimpse of Jesus' glory, his special relationship with the Father. From now on the disciples are believers, not just learners and companions. A second answer will emerge more gradually: see ahead on 3.22–36, and 4.1–42.

Turbulent Pilgrim (2.13–22)
The synoptic gospels report Jesus' temple cleansing quite late in the story, but John has this near the start. An effect of this early position is that we see other incidents in the light of this one. Jesus will be a renewing but disturbing presence, pointing his people's worship into fresh directions, constantly relating their festivals to his own ministry and purpose—just as he transformed the water of Jewish cleansing at Cana (2.6).

So the temple cleansing is a genuine protest: this building should not be a market (2.16). Yet it has a deeper connotation too. Jesus' zeal for God will kill him (2.17), and through death his body will be a new temple, a new place for earth to meet with God (2.21). But only when he is risen will this really make sense (2.22).

Blowing in the Wind (3.1–21)
Nicodemus is impressed by Jesus' signs (3.2), but this sort of faith can be superficial, and Jesus is wary of people who hold it (2.23–25). No wonder

the exchange that follows is full of misunderstandings. Nicodemus needs to go deeper, but he can make little of Jesus' talk about new birth (3.3–10), and he does not contribute to the conversation again. Jesus ends by speaking of light and darkness (3.19–21), as if to suggest that Nicodemus' nocturnal visit (3.2) was a cautious and evasive tactic. One day he will work for Jesus, before night falls (19.38–42). But he is not ready yet.

Bridal Path (3.22–36)
John the Baptist has given his testimony (1.8, 15, 32; 3.32). Now his work is done, and he is ready to step back. Here John casts himself as best man at a wedding, glad to see the groom getting all the attention. The bridegroom, of course, is Jesus. There is a biblical allusion too, to Old Testament texts that picture God as his people's bridegroom, calling them into a relationship of security and delight (Isaiah 54.4–8; 62.4f; Hosea 2.16–20). Jesus comes to fill this role, just as he took the bridegroom's role at Cana, in providing the wine.

Well Met (4.1–42)
This encounter with the Samaritan woman is a counterpoint to Jesus' strained interview with Nicodemus: a Jewish elder, and a lowly Samaritan; a man of status, and a woman alone; the two could scarcely be more different. Yet she gets the point, tells her neighbours, invites Jesus to stay, and launches a community of faith (4.29, 39–42). She meets Jesus in the clear light of day (4.6), while Nicodemus gropes in the dark.

This episode also picks up a couple of strands from earlier in John. At Jacob's well (4.5f), we see Jesus again as God's new Jacob, ready to renew Israel's life. Also — as wells had proved significant meeting places for couples (Gen 24; 29; Ex 2) — there is a hint of Jesus as the heavenly bridegroom, come to gather his people into intimate friendship with God. Yet he starts (some readers might have said) with the most unlikely person in the world — foreign, female, frayed, breaking all the safe stereotypes that Nicodemus so neatly met. And through her a church is born. God's faithful people, it seems, will be bigger than before, but without such neat boundaries. God will give the harvest (4.35–38) in unexpected times and places.

Seeing and Believing (4.43–54)
This is the first healing John describes. Others were surely implied earlier (2.23), and these have given Jesus a reputation in Galilee too (4.45). But this is a shallow faith (2.24f); these people's belief depends on seeing (4.48, where 'you' is plural). By contrast the sick child's father finds his way to faith, when he is still many miles from home (4.50). Belief, it seems, can come without sight (cf 20.29). Indeed a concern to see may even make it harder to trust.

John 5–9: 'Moses Wrote About Me'

These chapters extend over three Jewish festivals. In John 5 Jesus is in Jerusalem as pilgrim (5.1). John 6 is set at Passover-tide, in Galilee—on a hillside (6.1–3), and in the synagogue at Capernaum (6.59). And in John 7 Jesus goes to Jerusalem for the Feast of Tabernacles (7.2–10). After this there is no new indication of time or place until John 10.

The mood of these chapters is gloomier and harsher than before. Several times Jesus is threatened with arrest or harm (5.16–18; 7.1, 30; 8.37, 59), and some of his own responses are very sharp (5.44; 7.34; 8.39–47; 9.40f). Yet at each stage there is a note of hope and possibility, as Jesus invites people to believe (5.24), to eat and drink (6.51; 7.37f), to keep his word (8.31, 51) and to see (9.39).

Sabbath Journey (John 5)
The trouble with this healing (5.2–9) is that it happens on a sabbath. Both the man carrying his makeshift bed, and Jesus in carrying out the healing, have worked on a day of rest (5.10, 16). Jesus defends himself by beckoning his opponents into a new point of view. God works constantly, and he claims the right to do the same (5.17–21).

Jesus goes on to talk of judgment and witness. People have tried to judge him; yet God trusts him to be their judge. Their response to him will be the germ of God's eventual verdict on their living (5.22–30). For he is the hub of Israel's life with God, and he draws testimony from all around: from John the Baptist (5.33), from his own deeds (5.36), from God (5.37) and—most relevant for his opponents—from the Scriptures and Moses (5.39, 46). The reference to Moses will open up major themes in the chapters ahead. But Jesus' sabbath-breaking will pursue him too (7.23; 9.16) into some awkward and angry exchanges.

Indeed the frequent use of judicial language in John—testimony, truth, judgment, challenge and question—seems to portray Jesus' whole ministry as a contest, an extended two-way trial. Israel proves and tries Jesus and, within this process, the whole world is being tested by God. The eventual verdict will only come at the crucifixion, where 'the ruler of this world' will be judged (12.31; 16.11), as the one who is himself the truth is lifted up in glory (17.1).[5]

Bread of Heaven (John 6)
The next four chapters carry forward the reference to Moses (5.46). Bread, water and light were 'Exodus gifts'—manna from heaven (Ex 16), water from the rock (Ex 17), and a fiery pillar to lead the people (Ex 13.21). So now Jesus re-enacts Moses' ministry, against the background of Israel's two great Exodus festivals, Passover and Tabernacles. He is bread from heaven (6.35, 41), refreshment for the thirsty (7.37f), and light of the world (8.12; 9.5).

Jesus performs two signs in John 6, feeding five thousand (6.1–13), and walking on the water (6.16–21). Then we follow the reactions of the people. To start with they try to make Jesus king, but he will not have it (6.14f); only later will he carry that title (19.19). Later, when the crowd catches up with him, Jesus urges them to look behind the sign. He brings a new sort of nourishment—a permanent gift, not one that has to be endlessly repeated (6.26f; cf 4.14).

The people reply with a biblical text, 'He gave them bread from heaven to eat' (6.31).[6] They think of manna, but Jesus uses their words to turn the discussion to himself. He is the living bread for which the world hungers (6.32–48). He is God's gift, and in turn he will give himself, in the sacrificial separation of flesh and blood, so that many may eat and live (6.49–58). He is proving a controversial—but for some a compelling—teacher (6.59–71).

Maverick Messiah? (John 7)
Tabernacles (7.2) was an autumn festival, recalling the shelters in which Israel lived on the Exodus journey. It included water-pouring ceremonies, and against this background Jesus speaks of himself as the source of living water (7.37–39). The mention of Scripture (7.38) probably refers to two sets of texts: some which look back to the Exodus, and water springing from the rock (eg Neh 9.15; Ps 78.15f; 105.41); and others which look forward, to a river flowing from the Jerusalem Temple (Ezk 47.1–12; Zec 14.8). Jesus is a new source of life for the earth, both as God's new Temple, and as the leader of Israel's new Exodus.

Around all this is a lively debate about Israel's Messiah (7.26f, 31, 41f). Could he possibly be a Galilean? There is a little intervention by Nicodemus (7.50f): a man on the way, perhaps.

Truth and Light (John 8 and 9)[7]
In addition to water-pouring, Tabernacles was a festival of light, with great lamps in the Temple courts.[8] As he did with bread and water, Jesus applies this image to himself, and speaks of light and guidance for all who follow (8.12). A little later he repeats the claim (9.5). These sayings lead to protracted and fractious discussions—the first about identity, the second about sight and sin.

John 8.12–59 is the longest and angriest argument between Jesus and his opponents. They question his testimony (8.13), his relationship to God (8.19) and his identity (8.25). In return he challenges their authenticity as Jews—their relationship to Abraham (8.33–41) and to God (8.42–47). The root question is one of truth. Jesus' testimony and word are God-given and trustworthy (8.13–18, 26, 31f, 47, 51), and he says that those who do not see this will get stuck in sin, like slaves in Egypt (8.21–24, 34). But truth liberates, and the truth is in Jesus (cf 14.6). He offers a new kind of Exodus, if only people will trust him and embrace the freedom he brings (8.32–36).

John 9 is all about a healing of a blind man. But ultimately it concerns spiritual vision too, and sin (9.35–41). At the start Jesus brushes aside the question of whether the man or his parents had sinned (9.2f). By the time the question returns (9.34), the link between sickness and sin has been made differently. Jesus is dubbed a sinner, for healing on the Sabbath (9.16, 25). And he calls Pharisees sinners, for thinking they can see clearly (9.41). Light is a place for dealing with sin, but you have to come to it (cf 3.19–21); otherwise the darkness blinds you.

Throughout these five chapters Moses has been, both overtly and implicitly, a regular presence in the text. But from now on he is not mentioned again. John believed that—rightly understood—Moses' ministry pointed forward to Jesus (5.39–47). Yet for some Moses' teaching had become a cul-de-sac (9.28f). Only by turning to Jesus, the gospel claims, would God's people gain proper perspective on their tradition; otherwise it would frustrate and bind.

John 10–12: Coming King

Stricken Shepherd (John 10)
The first half of John 10 continues the preceding discussion, and reflects on the leadership that Jesus offers. The end of this conversation, showing once again 'a division' over Jesus (cf 7.12, 43), comes at 10.19–21. But there is also a forward movement in John 10. The theme of sheep and shepherding, which runs right through 10.1–30, relates to the Dedication festival (10.22), and pushes the narrative on towards the passion.

Dedication (10.22) commemorated the recovery of the Temple for Jewish worship, in 164 BC after three years of foreign control. The occasion stirred up thoughts of leadership and liberty. The original freedom-fighters had entered Jerusalem with 'palms and psalms' (1 Macc 13.51). What sort of leader might Jesus be? 'If you are Messiah, tell us' (10.24).

Jesus' talk of shepherding does indeed cast him as leader. It sets him in the tradition of David the shepherd-king, and offers a caring and sacrificial model for his own rule (10.11–18). He will lay down his life, and 'other sheep, not of this fold' will be gathered too (10.16)—a hint of Gentile mission to come.

In several ways John 10 anticipates events and themes ahead. One will die for many, and God's scattered flock will be gathered (11.50–52). A king rides into Jerusalem, with palm branches and singing (12.13). Gentiles are drawn to Jesus (12.20, 32). But first we see Jesus acting out the role of good shepherd, placing his own life in danger for his friend Lazarus.

On the Fourth Day (John 11)
Threats against Jesus have continued and indeed escalated (10.31–33, 39).

After getting out of danger for a while (10.40–42), he deliberately returns to the scene, for the sake of his friend (11.7–16). Life comes for Lazarus, because Jesus is ready to die.

Jesus speaks differently to the two sisters. With Martha, he talks of resurrection (11.21–27). When he meets Mary, he enters into her grief (11.32–37). He neither denies the hurt of death, nor accepts it as the end of life.[9] Finally he stands at the door of the tomb, like a shepherd at the gate of the fold, and brings Lazarus out to life (11.38–44).

The disciples' sense of danger was correct (11.8). Jesus is causing concern in high places. Caiaphas' attitude is expedient, at best. Yet still he manages to be prophetic (11.45–53). The Passover is near (11.55), and the Lamb must be sacrificed.

Prelude to Passion (John 12)

There are echoes of John 1 in this chapter, which may suggest a rounding off of the mission part of the gospel, as the focus narrows towards the passion. Notice, for example, angels and the Son of Man (1.51; 12.29, 34); Jesus as king (1.49; 12.13–15); light and darkness (1.4f; 12.35f, 46). Gradually the narrative loses pace, and Jesus' last short speech brings together many themes from the Book of Signs (12.44–50). He is ready to go forward to die.

John 12 is full of pointers to the passion. The anointing at Bethany is a kind of advance burial rite. In the family where he brought life, Jesus is marked out for his own funeral, as Mary joins Caiaphas in prophesying his dying (12.1–8). Then as Greeks enquire after him (12.20), Jesus speaks more fully about his cross.

The passion will be a scene of honour and glory (12.23), and of harvest too, from across the earth (12.20–24, 32). It will be a template for the disciples' commitment (12.24–26). And for Jesus, this is the culmination of all he has done. Always he was sustained by the Father's will and work (4.34; 5.36; 6.38; 10.25). Now, fully and finally, he will bring glory to the Father (12.27f), so that evil will be judged and conquered (12.31), and the nations drawn to praise (12.32).

The language of 'lifting up' (12.32) has many contact points in the OT. It casts Jesus as the Servant, who dies for the sins of others (Isaiah 52.13). Then it recalls (*via* John 3.14) the bronze serpent of Numbers 21: Jesus' death is healing and life-dealing. There is a hint too of the standard raised by Israel's king, for the world to gather round (Isaiah 11.10, 12; John 11.52; 12.20, 32).

The passion is rich in meaning. But it will be grim in detail. We must follow Jesus there.

The Jesus of Passion

4

John 13–16: Fellowship of Friends

These chapters show Jesus and his friends in private conversation, away from the sparring of public debate. There are shadows outside, and thoughts of hard times to come (13.2, 30; 15.18–16.4). But the chief note is of trust, fellowship and belonging. These are words to affirm and support. The conversation has four movements.

'He Loved His Own' (13.1–30)

The footwashing is an expression of love—Jesus' love for 'his own,' and God's love, which sends and sustains him (13.1–4). As he moves round the table with the basin, he acts out the whole course of the gospel. For Jesus has stepped aside from glory in 'the form of a slave' (*cf* Phil 2.7), 'laying down his garments' (13.4) as he will lay down his life (10.17f; 15.13). Only when his servant work is complete, and 'his own' are clean (13.5–11), does he take up his outer dignity (13.12; 17.4f). The footwashing stands for the incarnation, and for the end to which it leads—the cross.

> *The footwashing stands for the incarnation, and for the end to which it leads—the cross*

This is an example, too, for Jesus' followers to copy (13.12–17). Love is not just a gift. It is also a pattern, to be worked out in the humblest and plainest situations. Rooted in the Father's love for the Son (17.24–26), it spreads through the incarnation and crucifixion (3.16), into the common life of Jesus' friends (13.34; 15.12), 'that the world may know' (13.35; 17.23).

Sadly not all can receive this (13.11, 18–30). The shadowy figure of Judas Iscariot will always be harder to understand, both psychologically and theologically, than some more positive characters in the gospel. He fulfils Scripture (13.18), yet does so by serving evil (13.2). When he goes out, it is night (13.30). Jesus' ministry is passing into darkness (9.4; 12.35f).

'Going to the Father' (13.31–14.14)

In John, Jesus speaks often about 'going' — for example, 'going to him who sent me' (7.33; also 8.14, 21f; 14.28; 16.5, 10, 17). Here he explains what he means. The 'going' is a journey into glory (13.31–33), and a journey that Jesus must take alone, before others will be able to follow (13.36–38). It is both crucifixion and ascension—almost fused into one. For in Jesus' lifting up on the cross, where he completes the Father's mission (13.1; 19.30), is the glory of God and of heaven (17.1–5).

Jesus then gives three promises to the friends he leaves. In their love for one another, others will recognize his love (13.34f). There will be a re-union, a 'place' where they will be at home with Jesus (14.1–7). And even as he leaves, his power and presence will remain (14.12–14).

'Peace I Leave With You' (14.15–15.17)

Jesus does not leave his people alone. They will be held, in a two-way bond of commitment and care. He promises them love and peace (14.21, 27), and they are to show their love by keeping his commands (14.15, 21–24; 15.14). Yet this relationship is more than just imitation and memory. It has an organic quality—abiding, fruit-bearing (15.1–11), friendship (15.12–17).

All this is possible through the work of the Advocate—the Holy Spirit. Four short passages speak of him, and the titles 'Advocate' and 'Spirit' appear in each, as if to underline that these are one and the same person (14.16f, 26; 15.26; 16.7–15).[10] As Jesus leaves, the Spirit will come, to support and guide. He will continue what Jesus has done, and help the church follow what Jesus has taught, through difficult days ahead.

'In the World You Have Tribulation' (15.18–16.33)

Now comes an abrupt change of mood. In the fellowship of friends, the world has been almost shut out. But it will intrude again. As it has challenged Jesus and will crucify him, so the world will 'hate' Jesus' friends (15.18–21). This is still the world God loved, which Jesus' followers must meet with integrity and hope (3.16; 17.23). But it is a perverse and hostile place too, continually blanking out the presence of love (1.10; 15.22–24; 16.1–3).

There is a controversial edge to the work of the Advocate

So there is a controversial edge to the work of the Advocate. As he teaches the disciples, he will also show the world its error and need (16.7–15), and will do this—at least in part—through the church's positive testimony to its Lord (15.26f). The trial process that runs through John, the judicial contest between Jesus and the world, will continue even after Jesus has left.

There is dark realism in this portion of the gospel—but also the promise of light, reunion and gladness. Jesus will come back to his friends (16.16–24). When he dies they will be desolate, but after he has risen they will rejoice, and never again will they be alone. Bereavement is temporary; resurrection is permanent. The joy and peace that Jesus gives will never end (16.22, 33).

John 17: 'I am Praying for Them'

In the course of John's gospel this prayer is a bridge, linking the Farewell Discourses and the passion. Jesus has told his disciples about what is ahead, and very soon he will be taken into the hands of his enemies. This prayer offers both—his friends and his suffering—to God. Like a high priest, he prepares for sacrifice—to enter God's presence, by offering his own life.

The prayer is a great parabola, anchored at both ends in the eternal one-ness of Father and Son. It begins before all time, with Jesus sharing heaven's glory, and carrying the Father's authority into his work on earth (17.2–5). And it ends in the ultimate gathering of Jesus and his people, where they see his glory and know within them the love that binds Father and Son (17.24–26).

Along its curve, the parabola gathers up the people of Jesus, as an ever-widening company taken forward to glory. First Jesus prays for himself, for God's final honouring of his life and work (17.1–5). Then his thoughts move outward, to the people God gave him, among whom he has shared God's life and truth (17.6–19). Lastly he looks ahead, and prays for the larger church of the future (17.20–26).

The church is a people 'sent into the world' (17.11, 18), as Jesus was sent (17.3, 8). So he asks that their living may show the source of their life, by pointing back to him and to his sending by the Father (17.21, 23). This will be possible through unity and truth. Commitment to truth will mark the church as a holy people, loyal to God rather than to earthly values (17.16–19), and because of this others will believe (17.20). And their unity will

The church is a people 'sent into the world,' as Jesus was sent

display the life of Father and Son, in which it is grounded (17.11, 21), and through which it has been filled with love (17.26). This love is given supremely, as Jesus goes to die.

John 18–19: Lifted Up to Die

From the very start of the gospel, John directs readers' eyes towards the cross. Jesus is Lamb of God (1.29, 36). His zeal for God leads him to offer his body as a new temple (2.17–21). He 'must' be lifted up (3.14). His commitment to the Father's 'work' (4.34; 5.36) threatens him with danger and death (5.17f). He offers himself as flesh and blood (6.52–58). He is spared arrest, because his 'hour' is yet to come (7.30; 8.20). Because he knows the Father, he will lay down his life (10.15, 17). The crucifixion has been in view for a long time. Now, as he tells of it, John deliberately lays out not only events but also meaning. As the passion proceeds, we see Jesus first as shepherd, then as king and lastly as Lamb of God.[11]

'I am He' (18.1–27)

In the confusion in the garden Jesus guards his own (10.28; 18.8f), as a shepherd puts his body between the flock and approaching danger (10.11–15). The high-priest's 'courtyard,' where Peter follows, is the word used earlier for 'fold' (10.16; 18.15) — a shepherd's place. But Peter cannot truly follow yet (13.36–38); only later will he be a shepherd for Jesus (21.15–17).

Caiaphas too is a shepherd, as high-priest 'for that year' (11.51; 18.13). But this is only a shadowy copy of Jesus' eternal priesthood (17.1–5). Even as he dies, Jesus' seamless robe recalls Israel's priestly garb (19.23f; cf Ex 39.27). He is in every way his people's true leader — not despite his passion, but through it and because of it.

'So You are a King?' (18.28–19.16)

The words 'king' and 'kingdom' appear constantly through 18.33–19.5, and again in 19.12–22. Jesus is dignified but laconic, Pilate testy and confused. 'What is truth?' he asks (18.38). Truth incarnate stands before him, but Pilate has no spiritual compass to orient himself with. So the process runs on all morning, through evasion (18.38–40), brutality (19.1–3), impasse (19.4–7) and fear (19.8, 12), until it collapses into concession (19.14–16) and one last small stubbornness (19.22). The whole discussion — is Jesus a king, or is he not? — is settled by a scornful placard and Pilate's refusal to alter it.

'It is Finished' (19.17–37)

As Israel waits to eat the Passover (18.28), and lambs are slaughtered in the Temple, Jesus dies as God's great sacrifice. Just as Moses was instructed, the lamb is sacrificed with hyssop; his bones are not broken; nor is his body left to morning (19.29–36; cf Ex 12.8, 10, 46). This is the true feast of freedom, drawing into itself all earlier Passovers, of the ages and of this gospel. Here are God's new Temple (2.13ff) and living bread to feed on (6.4f, 51).

Once Jesus drew back from his mother; now he reaches out

A group of faithful women wait near the cross, Jesus' mother among them. Once Jesus drew back from her: 'his hour had not yet come' (2.4). But this is the 'hour' and he reaches out, to entrust her to his 'Beloved Disciple' (19.25–27). This disciple is a witness too. His testimony shapes the gospel's account (19.35), and we shall hear from him again.

The passion has run its course. Scripture has been fulfilled (19.24, 28, 36f), and prophecy too (18.14, 32). In some ways Jesus has been in command all along (18.6, 11; 19.11, 26f). He has completed his work for God, and even with his last breath, there is a hint that he releases the Spirit (19.30). Yet this has been an ugly, humiliating and painful death, and John has made its indignity and misery very clear (18.12, 22; 19.1–3, 18, 23f, 28). It was a real, physical, human dying (19.5, 33f), and Jesus has borne it alone (19.17). He is dead.

'There was a garden' (19.38–42)

The passion ends, as it began, in a garden (18.1; 19.41). The burial spices Nicodemus brings would be fit for a king (19.39). He has found his way, at last, into the kingdom (cf 3.3, 5). Even as Jesus is carried to his grave, a rich man discovers new life, before night falls (19.42).

John 20: Garden of Life

John 20 is about resurrection and response. Jesus is alive, and people are starting to believe it. Here are four main scenes in Jerusalem, two at Jesus' tomb (20.1–10, 11–18), and two in 'the house' (20.19–23, 26–29), with four followers at the hub of the action. In each pair of scenes, the person who is at first a little distant then becomes the centre of attention. For Mary wept 'outside the tomb' (20.11), while two male disciples went in to look (20.6–8). And Thomas 'was not with them' on the first Easter evening (20.24). Yet Peter and the Beloved Disciple fade out of the spotlight for a while. Only later, in Galilee, do we watch them encounter Jesus (21.1–23). Before then, the light of faith falls on Mary and Thomas.

Both of these come to faith after a moment of uncertainty and misunderstanding (20.14f, 25). And both have to face a tension between faith and sensory experience. For Mary sees, but she may not touch (20.17). And Thomas may touch (although in the event he does not need to), but then Jesus tells him that, ideally, belief should not depend on sight (20.29). These are not easy encounters nor stereotypical believers. Yet their faith is real—'My Master;' 'My Lord and my God' (20.16, 28)—and God uses it. Mary is witness to the apostles (20.18), and Thomas to the very purpose of the gospel (20.28).

Mary is witness to the apostles, and Thomas to the very purpose of the gospel

This whole chapter resonates with the beginning of John. The garden hints at creation renewed and humanity starting again. Thomas confesses Jesus as God (1.1; 20.28). A clear sight of God has been possible in Jesus; but once again faith will have to live without this (1.18; 20.29). Jesus stands among his people (1.26; 20.19, 26), asks what they seek (1.38; 20.15), and passes on the Spirit he has received (1.32f; 20.21–23). And as belief in Jesus brings new life, so John writes to kindle life in those who read (1.12f; 20.30f). For Easter is no enclosed event, safe behind locked doors and a neat conclusion. Rather the life of Jesus breathes through his followers (20.21–23), and this gospel of his signs points many to faith (20.30f). His people have work to do, care to give, and witness to bear.

John 21: Morning of a New Day

John 21 is an epilogue, pushing the gospel into the future. Yet it is by no means a disconnected postscript. It catches hints and hopes from the broad sea of John's narrative, to nourish the church for the long day ahead. There is a resonance with Jesus' earlier feeding—provision and distribution, and mastery of the water (6.1–21). There are echoes of the opening of John—'turned and saw them following' (1.38; 21.20); 'Simon, son of John' (1.42; 21.15–17); testimony (1.6–8; 21.24). But the important aspect of this epilogue is the way it brings Peter and the Beloved Disciple from the new light of Easter morning into key roles for the future.

Peter had wanted to lay down his life for Jesus, and then he collapsed into threefold denial (13.36–38; 18.15–27). Now, beside another charcoal fire (18.18; 21.9), Jesus probes him gently, three times over (21.15–17), calls him to be a shepherd, and promises that he will indeed lay down his life (10.11–18; 21.18f). Peter is restored and healed. As a man of action and impulse (21.7), he longs to be involved in Jesus' work. Now, thank God, his hopes and aspirations are not denied or destroyed. He is wanted, trusted and loved.

Beside Peter the man of action, the Beloved Disciple is a man of witness

Finally comes the Beloved Disciple, who sat with Jesus at dinner, waited at the cross, ran to the tomb, and recognized the Lord on the shore (13.23–26; 19.25–27, 35; 20.2–10; 21.7).[12] Here at the end the veil falls: this is his gospel; he is the witness who selected the material and told the story (21.24f). He was there, and his testimony is true. Beside Peter the man of action, the Beloved Disciple is a man of witness, steward of the story for the sake of the church to come.

Themes and Issues in John

5

We have touched on many important themes already, as we went through John's text.

Here are just a few of the issues that deserve more direct discussion.

John and the Other Gospels

John differs from the other gospels, as we noticed in the introduction. Beside the points mentioned there, John does not report, for example, Jesus' infancy, temptation, exorcisms or transfiguration. There is no list of the Twelve, nor do they go out on mission. The teaching is different too: there is more reflection, and less ethics; fewer parables, but a series of 'I am' sayings. Why is John so distinctive? Here is a rough sketch of four approaches. Most people who study John would favour some combination of these.

1 This gospel reflects experiences that John and his church had passed through. For example, some sayings about persecution may mirror hardships they faced (9.22; 15.18–16.4). Original teaching of Jesus could well have been overlaid and expanded, to meet pastoral needs in the decades that followed, and then written down in the gospel.

2 Much of Jesus' teaching is adapted in John. Key ideas are preserved but their presentation is changed. So John 3.3 might be a reworking of the saying in Mt 18.3; John 10 may reflect the parable in Lk 15.17; John 6.51–58 could arise from Mk 14.22–25. If John is a more considered gospel than the others, this is because he wanted above all to show the meaning of Jesus' deeds and words. This is a preacher's gospel. Early Christian thought about Jesus is woven into the story of what he did.

3 John had access to distinctive material. Some place-names are peculiar to John (Bethany beyond Jordan, Aenon near Salim, Bethzatha, Gabbatha), and these are one trace of his personal testimony, to events that he knew about. There may also be a link between the style of Jesus' teaching and the amount of John's gospel that is set in Jerusalem—if Jesus used a more argumentative style with the learned men of the city than in rural Galilee.

4 John wrote to supplement one or more of the synoptics. If he takes for granted, say, Mark's material, he could have worked around this, expanding it both with other incidents and with indications of its meaning.[13]

All of this leads us on, to consider the purpose for which John wrote.

John's Purpose and Audience

John explains why he wrote: 'that you may believe that the Christ, the Son of God, is Jesus, and in believing have life in his name' (20.31). But we do not know quite what he meant, whether he wrote principally to bring people to faith, or to sustain those who were Christians already.[14]

Indeed parts of this gospel could fit with either of these aims. There is plenty of material about the church (John 13–17; 21). But there are also direct invitations to the reader, to take up what Jesus offers (4.13f; 6.35; 8.12; 14.6). So John may well have had a double purpose: to support Christians in their own faith, and to offer a resource that would help them tell others.

John's core audience — the ethnic context in which he wrote — was probably Jewish. This gospel draws extensively on OT material, and deals so fully with Jewish worship, that it would scarcely have been well understood by someone from right outside that culture. Certainly the prologue has affinities with Greek thought. But the Jewish background is much broader.

John and Judaism

Although John's gospel is deeply rooted in Jewish tradition, it has often caused disquiet in places where Jews and Christians meet. Indeed some Christians, over the centuries, have used this gospel to foster anti-semitic views and deeds. The centre of this difficulty is the frequency and tone of the word 'Jews' in John.

At times this word means roughly what it means today (2.6; 4.9, 22; 6.4) — Jewish people in general. But elsewhere it refers more narrowly to Jerusalem and its religious leaders: 'Judeans,' would be more accurate than 'Jews' (1.19; 2.18; 5.10). And on several occasions when Jesus is in Jerusalem and 'the Judeans' are in view, we meet scenes of controversy, enmity and anger (5.16; 7.1; 8.48; 11.8; 19.14f).

This animosity in the gospel has persuaded some people that there was a similar ill-feeling in John's own situation, that he was writing from outside organized Judaism, a few decades after Jesus, and allowing his gospel to reflect quarrels of his own time. Although the church had Jewish roots, there had been, it is suggested, a split with the wider Jewish community, so that John now looked back in anger across a great gulf. The parting, which may have been triggered by a change in synagogue regulations (9.22; 12.42; 16.2), caused Christians to use language of enmity and blame about Jewish neighbours. A good deal of this was crystallized in John's text (8.39–47; 9.39–41).

I am not wholly convinced by this explanation, for three reasons. First, from the birth of the church, there was tension with wider Judaism (Acts 6.8–15; 12.1–3; 2 Corinthians 11.24). Christians lived with this, without breaking contact. Second, polemical language was used more readily in that era than in Western religious discussion today. You could express an opinion strongly (as OT prophets did), without this reflecting or causing a total break in relationship. Third, even the harshest language in John is not far away from words of challenge, invitation and hope.

John surely wrote in a setting where Christians (most of them messianic Jews) had disagreed strongly with some Jewish neighbours. Yet contact had not been broken, and even the polemic of this gospel probably had a more constructive purpose than is often thought. The world where many had opposed Jesus was still the world God loved. John would have said the same about Israel, the people to which he himself belonged.

John and Christian Worship

In John, the material and the spiritual interlock. 'The word became flesh' (1.14). So John has been a rich source of reflection for sacramental theology. But agreed conclusions have been difficult to draw.

On one hand, John does not mention directly either Jesus' baptism or his institution of the Lord's Supper, and he explicitly says that Jesus did not baptize (4.2). He does not show, in the way the synoptics do, the ministry of Jesus as the launch-pad for Christian sacraments. On the other hand, it is striking how often we meet water, bread or wine at the very heart of an episode (eg John 3.5; 6.11; 13.5; 15.1; 19.34). And John was clearly a subtle and careful author, who sometimes expected his audience to read between the lines.

I think these two insights connect. John saw Jesus as the great intersection of the material world and the life of God. Out of his incarnation came signs—healing, feeding, and so on—and these found their full value when they were seen to point beyond themselves, to Jesus' life and death. The same may apply with our Christian sacraments. If John alludes indirectly to these, this is because they too beckon us to look behind them. As water and blood flowed from the crucified body of Jesus (19.34), baptism and communion become God's signs to us when they draw us, over and again, to the cross.

John and God

In John's gospel we see the outline of the church's belief in God as Trinity. The source of Jesus' mission is the Father, who sent him and to whom he returns (3.34; 14.28; 16.27; 17.13). Jesus serves the Father's will and work (4.34; 6.38; 10.37), speaks the Father's words (3.34; 7.16; 12.49), and seeks the Father's glory (5.44; 7.18).

Many texts speak in exalted ways about Jesus' relationship with the Father. Only occasionally is Jesus called 'God' (1.1; 20.28); yet the Father grants him equal status (5.22f); he is trusted by the Father (3.35); Father and Son dwell within one another (10.38; 14.7–11; 17.21). The text distinguishes the two clearly, when the talk is of Jesus' coming and leaving. But as he reveals God in his mission, Jesus is intimate, equal and even identical (5.17–19; 10.30, 33; 14.10; 15.23). The gospel underlines this in two particular ways.

One is Jesus' pre-existence, his heavenly companionship with the Father before his coming. 'He was before I was,' says the Baptist (1.15, 30). Jesus can represent God, because he has been with God and has seen and known God (1.1–3, 18; 3.10–13; 6.46; 7.29; 8.58; 17.5). He brings into his incarnation the life and insight of heaven.

There are also the seven 'I am' sayings (bread, 6.35; light, 8.12 and 9.5; door, 10.7, 9; shepherd, 10.11, 14; resurrection and life, 11.25; way, truth and life, 14.6; vine, 15.1, 5).[15] These reflect a number of individual OT themes. But they also make an impact as a group, drawing onto Jesus the name revealed to Moses (Ex 3.14). They resonate too with Isaiah, where the Lord reminds Israel, 'I am he' (41.4; 43.10, 13, 25; 46.4; 48.12): he alone is first and last, maker and saviour. None ranks with him. John's gospel affirms this of Jesus.

The relationship between Father and Son is energized by the Spirit. As Son, Jesus bears the Spirit, who rests on him, inspires what he says, and reaches out through him to give new life (1.32f; 3.34; 6.63). He passes on the Spirit to others too (1.33; 7.37–39; 20.22), but this promise is only fully realized after he is 'glorified' (7.39). At that point, Father and Son are so closely and fully united that the Spirit is sent by both (14.16, 26; 15.26; 16.7). So as the Spirit guides the church into all truth, the life of Father and Son is known (16.12–15).

The life of the Trinity is a life of love. In love God gave Jesus. In death Jesus gave himself, and his dying expressed not only the love of Father and Son for the world (3.14–16; 6.51; 15.13), but also the love that binds Father and Son together (10.17f; 14.31). Now he draws his friends into the fellowship of this love, grounded in his own union with the Father (15.10f; 17.24–26), and enabled by the gift of the Spirit (14.15–17; 16.12–15). And in love the church trusts Father, Son and Spirit as one God.

Preaching and Teaching from John 6

Reading from John

Matthew, Mark and Luke each contribute heavily in one year of the Revised Common Lectionary, and are almost silent for the other two. John, by contrast, appears every year, with a run of about ten Sundays from Lent to Trinity. Outside these periods, John is used quite sparsely.[16]

About half of John is listed for Sunday reading. The controversies of John 5, 7 and 8 hardly show at all. John 13, 18 and 19 are little used on Sundays, but are listed for Holy Week, where they can speak powerfully. Most of the rest appears, including all seven 'I am' symbols, and many well-known incidents and conversations.

It rarely comes in tight gospel order. There are some continuities: the encounters of John 3, 4, 9 and 11 in Lent of Year A, for example; and five weeks of John 6, in the summer of Year B. Yet most of the connections from week to week come through themes and seasons, rather than through close ordering in the text.

Preaching from John

Many preachers find depth in John. There are texts and passages for sermons on all sorts of big issues: faith, hope and love, for example; new life, discipleship, vision, evangelism; the cross, the Spirit, the Trinity. How can we approach all of this, in a way that is faithful to John as a whole gospel? Here are four thoughts:

- John's entire theology is bound to the 'Christ event' — the incarnation, ministry, death and resurrection of Jesus. Whatever we preach from John should pass through this vortex. The church has no life and no message, apart from Jesus. Faith, prayer, mission, love and worship are possible because of this historical figure. 'The word became flesh.' God communicated with the world through a particular person. Preach well from John to remind people — because we forget — that all our living finds its centre and orientation in Jesus.

- John's story is drawn to the cross from the start, and in more than a dozen ways it outlines the meaning and glory of Jesus' death. The crucifixion was both tragedy and triumph, self-giving and necessity, honour and degradation, death and life. To preach John is to come often to Golgotha, yet regularly to sense that we have not come by quite this way before. Help people to see the cross from many aspects. We need these in different seasons of our lives.

- This gospel uses language in two distinctive and distinct ways. Some is polarized—darkness and light, truth and falsehood, death and life, love and hate, whereas in other places the discussion is quite subtle, turning an idea in more than one direction—flesh, for example (6.53, 63)—or exposing a second layer of meaning, to help someone get past a point of misunderstanding (3.4–7). Most preachers, I suspect, incline to one or other of these two very different approaches. While some of us think instinctively of polarity and challenge, others prefer subtle or half-hidden insights. Perhaps John urges us, whatever our natural style, to strike a balance in the way we tell the gospel. Help people to think deeply; remind them too that faith involves critical choices and tough commitments.

- Finally, this is a gospel of love, love which has an endless and eternal source in God, and flows out through Jesus and you and me. Let us preach it lovingly, and live it lovingly. Footwashing—humble service—is part of that. Preach with hands and heart, as well as with words. God did.

Teaching from John

How could you get a taste of John in a few sessions, with a school class, church Bible study or Lent group? Here is one suggestion:

Obstacles and Opportunities

The characters in John often have to overcome something in themselves—misunderstanding, prejudice, fear, failure—when they deal with Jesus. Take half a dozen people who had to do this, and look at their encounters with Jesus. Ask what held them back, what (might have) helped them, how they ended up, and (if your group can cope with this) how much of this person we see in ourselves. Try, for example, Nicodemus (3.1–21; 7.45–52; 19.38–42), the woman at the well (4.1–42), Pilate (18.28–19.22), Mary Magdalene (20.1–18), Thomas (11.16; 14.5; 20.19–29) and Simon Peter (13.36–38; 18.15–27; 21.1–19).

Resources on John

7

Books on John appear ceaselessly. This is just a selection. There are plenty of good and helpful works beyond these.

Commentaries

Big Commentaries

C K Barrett, The Gospel according to St John (SPCK, 2nd ed, 1978). A weighty and learned commentary from a shrewd and clear Methodist professor.

G R Beasley-Murray, Word Biblical Commentary (Word Books, 2nd ed, 1999). Careful and informed; moderately evangelical. 'Explanation' sections condense much of the detail.

R E Brown, Anchor Bible Commentary (Doubleday, 2 vols, 1966–70). A major academic commentary by an able Roman Catholic scholar. Dating a little, but very clear and full.

D A Carson, The Gospel according to John (IVP, 1991). Solid. Conservative. Attentive to questions of history, and concerned to explain the text.

A T Lincoln, Black's New Testament Commentary (Continuum, 2005). Academically up-to-date. Critical and theological.

F J Moloney, Sacra Pagina: The Gospel of John (Liturgical, 2005). By an academic, for the church. Attentive to John's narrative and its effect on the reader.

B Witherington, John's Wisdom (WJKP, 1995). Regards wisdom as a key to the gospel. 'Bridging' sections open up angles for exposition.

Smaller Commentaries

R Burridge, People's Bible Commentary (Bible Reading Fellowship, 1998). Meant for new preachers or house-group leaders; useful for daily reading too.

K Grayston, Epworth Preacher's Commentary (Epworth Press, 1990). A series designed to help Methodist lay preachers.

C Kruse, Tyndale Commentary (IVP, 2003). A responsible evangelical series, which always aims to explain the text.

J H Neyrey, New Cambridge Bible Commentary (CUP, 2007). Textual detail and theological depth, from an American Roman Catholic professor.

M Stibbe, Readings (Sheffield, 1993). Helpfully different. Attends to the narrative as story; spots links and themes at every stage.

W Temple, Readings in St John's Gospel (Macmillan, 1940). Deep but readable theology, by a one-time Archbishop of Canterbury.

N T Wright, John for Everyone (SPCK, 2 vols, 2002). Lively, learned and lucid, from the Anglican Bishop of Durham. Divided for daily reading.

Books About John

R B Edwards, Discovering John (SPCK, 2003). A clear and thoughtful student introduction, by an experienced university teacher.

W J Harrington, John: Spiritual Theologian (Columba Press, 1999). A Roman Catholic series, showing how the gospels have a message today.

A-J Levine (ed), A Feminist Companion to John (Continuum, 2 vols, 2003). Female characters and women's perspectives in John's gospel. Quite academic.

B Lindars, John: NT Guide (Continuum, 1991). A lucid and serious student introduction.

D Moody Smith, The Theology of the Gospel of John (Cambridge University Press, 1995). A volume by a John specialist, in a series suited for second-level university work.

S S Smalley, John—Evangelist and Interpreter (Paternoster, 2nd ed 1997). Judicious, clear, quite deep, and balanced. Suitable for second-level students.

Web Resources

The Grove web site (www.grovebooks.co.uk) has more 'Comments on Commentaries': go to Biblical Studies Bulletin.

Some other sites are consistently helpful:

www.ntgateway.com—an academic site, with access to plenty of material for others too

www.lectionary.org—exegesis of the lectionary texts

www.textweek.com—a wide variety of material for use in worship

Notes

1   The terms 'Book of Signs' and 'Book of the Passion' come from C H Dodd, *The Fourth Gospel* (Cambridge: University Press, 1953). The title 'Book of Glory' was coined by R E Brown, *Anchor Bible Commentary* Vol 1 (New York: Doubleday, 1966).

2   Like John, the Letter to the Hebrews also speaks of Jesus from the very outset without mentioning his name, until 2.9. Was John deliberately giving a mixed audience room to reflect, to engage their curiosity, to mesh his words with their own concerns and thoughts, before he showed his hand? In Britain today, with a thinner Christian background than a few decades ago, this kind of 'suspense writing' in Scripture may have a particular contribution to make—even in some Christmas services.

3   By this reckoning the first five days begin at 1.19, 29, 35, 41, 43; 'the third day' (2.1) moves us on from day five to day seven.

4   B Witherington's commentary, *John's Wisdom*, explores this connection very fully: especially pp18–27. He notes a number of parallels between this gospel and Jewish wisdom writing from the inter-testamental period (*eg* Wisdom of Solomon 10–19; and Ecclesiasticus [aka Sirach] 24).

5   A T Lincoln, *Truth on Trial* (Peabody: Hendrickson, 2000) explores this trial theme in depth.

6   These words match Ps 78.24 almost exactly. But they may also refer to Exodus16.4.

7   The account of the woman taken in adultery (John 7.53–8.11) is quite credible. In several respects it seems typical of Jesus. But it was probably not original to John's gospel. Most early manuscripts of John lack it, and some ancient manuscripts include it at a different point in John, or indeed in Luke. Probably it was handed on in Christian tradition for a few generations, without being included in a written gospel. Only subsequently was a place found for it in the text.

8   The late-second-century Mishnah (Sukkah 4 and 5) has more detail about Tabernacles.

9   This is surely a balance to strike in our own caring for bereaved people. But Jesus' conduct indicates the need for sensitivity. There is a time for hope and a time for tears, and even in one family these arrive at different times for different people.

10 'Advocate' appears in the NRSV. Some other English translations (Comforter, Counsellor) underline the Spirit's support and encouragement. But these texts have a tough side too, as the Spirit defends the people of Jesus in a hostile world. There is no wholly satisfactory translation. No single English word catches all the nuances of the Greek word 'Paraclete.'

11 I learned this, and much else, from Mark Stibbe's *Readings* commentary (Sheffield Academic, 1993).

12 The Beloved Disciple may also appear at 1.35–40, and 18.15f. On John 21, and on the Beloved Disciple more generally, see R Bauckham, *Jesus and the Eyewitnesses* (Grand Rapids: Eerdmans, 2006), chapters 14–16. Bauckham reckons this man was John the Elder (not John son of Zebedee). He also argues that the reason John's gospel is more reflective than the synoptics is that an eyewitness wrote it. Eyewitnesses were expected to write with insight into the meaning of events. They had been there and would understand.

13 This view is worked out in some detail by R Bauckham, 'John for readers of Mark,' in Bauckham (ed), *The Gospels for all Christians* (Grand Rapids: Eerdmans, 1998) pp 147–171.

14 One reason for uncertainty is that the word 'believe' comes in two different grammatical forms in the ancient manuscripts of 20.31. One reading (*pisteusete*) may well mean 'come to believe,' implying an evangelistic purpose. The other (*pisteuete*, just one letter shorter) has a sense more like 'go on believing,' which would be more pastoral.

15 There are also 'I am' sayings without predicates at John 4.26; 6.20; 8.24, 28, 58; 13.19; 18.5–8.

16 For further detail, see the Grove website.